GREEN WHISTLE

GREEN WHISTLE

by

David Koenig

Wm Caxton Ltd

P.O. Box 1050, Evanston, IL 60204-1050

First published in 1988 by
Wm Caxton Ltd, P.O. Box 1050, Evanston, IL 60204-1050.

Early versions of the poems "Gravel Bones In Waltz Time,"
"Green Whistle," and "Wheelchair" were published in *Passage*,
v.6 [1980], *Ariel* v.1 [1983], and *Ariel* v.4 [1985], respectively,
periodical publications of the Triton College Press, 2000
Fifth Avenue, River Grove, IL 60171.

10 9 8 7 6 5 4 3 2 1

Library of Congress, Cataloguing in Publication Data:

Koenig, David, 1944-
    Green Whistle / by David Koenig.
        p.   cm.
    ISBN 0-940473-05-4 : $10.00
    I. Title.
    PS3561.03343G74   1988
    811'.54--dc19   88-10941
                                                        CIP

ISBN 0-940473-05-4

To my daughter Felice; to my father
and mother, my brother Steven, my
stepson Louis, and all who helped; to
the talented and loving editor and
partner of this creation, my wife Joyce;
and to the Great Creator.

Table of Contents

DEATHS AND BIRTHS

First Poem On A Father's Death

Not stone any more
The flesh on your bones,
Only gentle loam,
Warm to the touch,
Bound for the earth,
Soil unsoiled,

You sailed in your white shroud, smooth,
The hull of your ship
Slipped down
Through troughs
Of one-time sea sediment,
Now no impediment.

Gravel Bones In Waltz Time

Burrowing down
To what's happening in the dirt
Through which you sank,
(How deep is six feet?),
In the woodenness,
Woundedness,
Shapes are forming
In my mourning mind,
Changing whatever is
Down there of your body,
More than insects and worms
Could advance
Your dance nuances,
Out of (or up from?)
Your coffin boards, until
Finally I enter
My own countenance
Of where you are,
A Viennese star
In the dark, Illinois earth sky,
Past gravity's warping
You float,
Suspended
In your grave,
Gravel bones
In waltz time,
Counting.

Father, The Muscle Man

You did not have to seem so strong,
Twisting yourself into poses
Like many bows on a package,
Promising much, but yielding little,
You did not have to hold yourself
    so tight,
I with my blunt scissors
Just wanted to get inside.

You did not have to seem so big,
Towering yourself into triangles
Like many pyramids on a desert,
Promising from a distance,
    but hard to reach.
You did not have to be so mysterious,
A dry stone sphinx,
I, not good at riddles, just wanted
    to drink you in.

But it was worse for you,
Twitching under the tension,
Wasn't it something like muscle man
The inmates called one clearly dying
In the German camps?
You did not have to disguise yourself
    as electrified wire,
I, working clumsily on our escape,
Just wanted to keep you
From your own dark light.

A Seed, Though Seldom Watered

Over your rough and solid wall
You peeped, a shy but constant
Lover to us all,
Your love was gold, though stained.

A grain of love once given
Grows when we in coffins lie,
Yours to me, mine to my child,
A seed, though seldom watered,
Can grow wild.

For Felice Without Words
(To An Infant Daughter)

Felice without words.
I would need your voice
To tell the softness
Of your cheeks without teeth,
Tune of tender vowels
In turning feather torso,
Soft lids, lashed light,
Eyes, blue beacons searching
To worlds without harm,
Down-sheltered skull,
Filmy arms fanned
By your own clear breathing,
Cycle of churning legs,
Sweetmilk skin,
Hands far feeling
And learning life.

The Strongest Part of the Sky
(Answers To A Child's Questions
After A Trip To The Carnival)

"What is the strongest
Part of the sky?
The sun, the moon, or the stars?"

The strongest
Part of the sky?
It fell to earth
Last night
As carnival lights.
The sun and moon rode around
On mechanical steel,
The stars spun the ferris wheel
Into pink, yellow, and blue cotton candy.

"What if the sun and moon and stars
Would fight one night
Like tigers and lions?
Who would we want to win?"

Birds might choose the sun,
Fish the moon,
And the man from the hills
Who ran the ferris wheel,
Squinting out over the tall grass,
Still a hunter under iron planets,
Would he choose the stars?

Is he the strongest
Part of the sky,
Turning the world
With his lever
So that all the planets fall
In our eyes,
Until again
They rise?

The Dream Of Being Remembered
Until The End Of Time
(for Felice)

"The dark is on my eyes, Daddy,
April died today.
I miss April.
Where did she go?
Is she coming back?
Who will she look like?
Will she come back as a little girl?
Is April down in the ground all alone?
Is her mother and father with her?
Is she close to them?
How will April eat?
How did she get into the ground?

When am I going to die?
When are you going to die, Daddy?
When I go into the ground
Will there be people with me?
Will Mommy go into the ground
        with me?
Will you?
What happened to April?
Did she forget to take her medicine?
April won't come back for a long time.
I won't ever die,
Then I won't have to go
Into the ground.
Will you love me
When I'm in the ground?"

A Father's Love Yearns

To hold you so close
That our hearts make yellow light,
Like butter in a churn,

A father's love yearns.

To wake you from sleep,
A rooster looking for your light,
Like dawn through cracks in barns,

You burn in my arms.

Sleeping Beauty

We were on our way
To see Sleeping Beauty,
But you pulled my arm.
It seemed a duty to stop
And watch you gather Autumn leaves
From downtown doorways.
It seemed absurd
To collect things so common
On a Sunday morning,
But no harm
In making bouquets
Of what others did not want.

So I sighed,
And settled down to watch you pick
The season's windfall
In your little hands,
Already becoming skilled at collecting,
Just three Autumns old.

"Sit down, Daddy," you said.
We sat on the curb
And gathered leaves,
Examining how no leaf
Is just one color,
And in every green
Sleeps two others.

Spider Sonata

Five year old
Spiderwoman
Unravels
My cassettes
And spins
Shining filaments
From room to room,
Table to chair to bed.

Those tapes will never
Play music again,
But write your
Spider score
My talented insect,
The urge to record
Is just the urge to connect.

DIVORCES

Battered Hands

She would not wash
From her hands, my daughter,
The cookie batter
She kneaded with me today,
But laughing,
Thrust them into my mouth,
One at a time, in a twinkling,
Five, five-year-old fingers,
Five sweet, slender stalks,
That who but a parent can measure,
Having gardened them from seed.

I could not wash
From my eyes, with tears,
The sight of those hands,
The taste and feel
From my mouth,
Where words
Cannot escape to say
How a father feels
When, once divorced,
He loses all right
To live with his child,
Or even to keep her
Within a thousand miles
Of his battered hands.

Space Heater

Suddenly the old-fashioned coil
Glows orange, and I am
My daughter's age again,
Back in my childhood bathroom,
Where this heater seemed
To make the whole world warm,
Where a mother and father could
Keep one far from harm.
A silent radiant fireplace,
This old blue hearth once again
Performs the miracle
Of heating space.

Archimedes' Bicycle

Unsteady and high,
Less wise than the sage
Of my first bike,
Almost middle aged,
I prepare for flight.
The street lands
Buildings and trees in my eyes,
Pavement in my groin and hands.
I smell restaurants,
The wind invites me to the lake.
In Spring aloft again,
I ache with the muscular waves,
With my child seated behind
Singing like a kite in the wind,
I fly, suspended on wheels,
Balancing like Archimedes,
Moving the world
From slightly above,
Levered along
As if by a goal,
As if by a love.

At The Zoo

I go to the zoo differently
Today at middle age,
See the fierce-hearted animals
Inside their ribbed cages
Are not, as I once thought,
Mere good-natured illustrations
From children's books,
Their home, size and age
Each inscribed on a laminated page.

No, these winter-mangey beasts,
Underneath their lethargy,
Still dream of killing at home,
In the old way, for the old reasons.
The Indian python
Big around as a woman's waist,
Is that thick and twenty feet long
For a purpose long forgotten
In its molded plastic prison.
Who can know
What jungle of woeful monsters
He measured out to survive in?
The same for the cobra's poison parasol,
Gorilla's squat, stone-cross spine.

No, never underestimate
The vacant cage of stares,
Perhaps seeing through the bars
Those early animals
On the children's balloons,

Smiling green frogs, pink panthers,
Patinaed on one side of helium,
The other side a shiny foil mirror
Handed down to children
By parents who know
Love does not glide
Like a seal's side wrist-flick.

Back at the zoo,
Still full of old rages.

Wild Horse

Say whatever you want for a life time,
But say that for now I am,
At this moment, grand.
Remember me from this time on,
Not as the song I would not sing,
But as a one-time fling.
Say, he threw out
The heart that did not sting,
That did not smart
And beat in his throat
When just one note was played,
One word sighed, to stay or fly away,
He did not wait
For time to have its day.
Say of me, he was here
Shouting death at his fears,
Booked flight to foreign solitude,
Then raged like a wild horse
Hard hastening home.

Rain

Go out and catch
The rain,
Let go the good grain
Of your door, and sail
Past port of blossomed bush
To where the storm
Will push the hair from your eyes
And you cry:
My life,
An old tree blighted,
Its leaves now hateful to my sight,
I catch the rain
In slipping hand-hatches
Of light,
I do not flee
This heaven-flooding,
That cuts my life in twain,
And twain again,
No end of these hail points.
At last at home I stand,
The sun now sloping
Through the leaves
Onto this stranger's cane,
The countless storm sustained.
Oh, may this wet-clothed,
Birth-peeled body
Brief remain.

Green Whistle

The winter moon brought
Me back to the campus tonight,
(It's always something,)
What do I go there looking for?
Looking for me, of course,
Twenty years younger,
Who believed those slender girls,
Swaying hiplegged down the sidewalk,
Could be a permanent comfort,
That those thin,
Bearded teaching assistants
With the handsome faces and fine hands
All had elegant careers ahead of them.
I was one of those bearded faces.
What am I now?
A campus Jesus
In blue-jeans and torn orange ski jacket,
Dead-ended, alone,
Watching this full moon coat
The gingerbread Victorian English building
With inedible sugar,
(I once believed in it,)
And spent twenty years plastering
Picture post cards
On the kiosk of a career,
Here, where the wind's icy knife
Whittles them away, one at a time,
With leaves from the trees.

The moon, which I still follow blindly,
Like every woman's shining button
From the darkness

Of walking folds of cloud
Suddenly comes for a minute clear,
And I see twenty years
Drifting silently away,
Disturbed by nothing more
Than an occasional red airplane light
Puttering like a row boat
Through the sky over the lake,
Twenty years of quaint attempts
To fix a place for myself with others,
(I can't remember
Exactly how I planned it,)
But walking here along the frozen lake,
Alone except for a steel-hearted jogger
And a student photographer
Of the moon,
Was not what I planned,
Nor that I would like being alone,
Free to imagine what I might become
Or what might come next,
Still afraid of the two old men
In the Chinese restaurant
On Davis Street,
Afraid that one of them is me,
But whether it is or not,
Willing to let the moon
Turn into a hot, white cup of tea,
Held in the hands of a boy
The wind has whittled,
From a brown branch
Down to a green whistle of joy.

MORTALITIES

A Clap Of Quiet Thunder
(for a mother's suicide)

Like a frail queen
You lie down
Under the silver bumper,
Car turned on,
Garage door shut.

Like a queen
You lie down
In make-up and jewelry,
On two blankets,
With pillow, slippers,
And a glass of water.
The well-tuned engine
Makes music for you,
And gas perfumes your sleep.

The car chokes off
As death finally awakens you
To your journey,
Like a clap of quiet thunder
In an empty tomb.

Ricocheted Crochet
(for my mother)

We, who wanted you
To try a little longer,
Forgot the crocheted coat hangers,
Hospital-volunteer hours,
Television-triggered lovers
In your solitary room.

Radio-active half-life
Of all you baked
Ticking in the kitchen,
Stored-up energy in beds you made
Building pressure like blankets of coal.

We who wanted you
To try harder, hang on longer,
Now find in our closets
Tangled rainbows
Of your ricocheted crochet.

Message From A Dream,
Attempting To Save A Mother

Walk with her,
Early in the morning
And late at night.
See with her
The rise of the sun
And the rise of the moon.
And when a moment comes,
When the world is as beautiful
As the world can get,
Then tell her the meaning
Of life as you know it.
Do this
And you will have done
The most
That you can possibly do.

In Those Lethal, Gorgeous Fumes

Frau Adele Bloch-Bauer
Sits patiently in Vienna
At the turn of the century,
While the great Gustav Klimt
Paints her in gold.
She does not suspect
That her portrait will be the one,
Now that her century has grown old,
To tell me who it is
I have been in love with
For all these years.

I regret to inform you,
Frau Bloch-Bauer,
That our golden Vienna
Threw out its every Jew
A short while after you died,
So I was born in American farm land,
Not knowing that the woman I loved,
In the person of my mother,
Was really you, Frau Adele Bloch-Bauer,
Viennese, Jewish, almost aristocrat . . .
(As Herzl warned), almost Viennese.

Poor Herr Klimt, no Jew himself,
Tried to show the golden city,
In his paintings, what was coming,
That government is not
A pleasant operetta,
And morality no evening at the theater,
Woman not a circus animal
Without a cage
That man can show anywhere unscathed.

Poor subversive Klimt,
The academics and politicians thought him
To be after their jobs . . . not
Under those painted
Gold hair combs,
After that black tangle
Truth.

But Frau Adele, (if I may,)
There you sit,
While Gustav fills in
The black and gold rectangles,
Thousand pyramids and eyes
Of your brocade dress and room,
Your walls becoming clothes,
Your clothes walls,
Fragile, dark-eyed insect,
In your golden tomb.

As Gustav plies
His father's ancient trade
Of gold engraving,
You and your city, Jerusalem,
Die and are reborn
In those lethal, gorgeous fumes.
Oh Mother, what we loved
Was so beautiful,
And so much ruin.

Coronary
(for a friend)

These two diseased arteries now are
The only crown around your heart,
The garland that serves as wreath
For all you have achieved.

This once-luminous red circle, that bound
The sun, your heart, around,
You, a man alone in a hospital room,
Is now the blue halo of your waning
    moon.

A Story For Dennis

Dennis,
I didn't write anything
When Bill died,
But you are the second
Shave-headed man
I didn't know well
To leave us this year.
Could it be
You both trimmed your hair
To hear death coming,
Or to see
With nothing in your eyes
That storybooks lie . . .
That no one
With a kind, or deep heart,
Dies?

My Death Is Blue

My death is deep inside me
And it is blue.
It is as unruffled as an ocean
Without a single ship or wave,
It is as continuous and smooth
As a robin's egg.
It is as constant and dark-centered
As the love in my daughter's eyes,
It is as unclouded and deep
As a summer night.

Cold Bookstore

The cold bookstore
Curls my fingers
Like pages.
My two hands
An aching scroll,
I read poems,
Some good,
But have time
Only for ones
That overcome the cold to say,
Like the blue ink veins
In my shrinking hands,
That something warm
Still flows.

The bookstore,
Full of windows,
Leaks mid-winter
Among the cool
White sheaves.
I resign myself to one.
The owner apologizes
For temperature
She cannot control,
But it has helped me choose,
And leave.

Some Desert Night

The camels spread out at dusk,
Set their silhouettes across the sky
Along the highway.
We see them leaving
Around great curves in the road,
Their eyes gleaming,
Carrying their towering loads.
They are the Semi's,
Half truck, half train,
Pulling out onto the highway
Around the ramp
From the all-night truck stop
Where we stand,
Stripped of our ailing car
As if by some sure hand.

The sun is setting on Illinois
Sand-hills of hazy wheat,
While my daughter and I wait
To be picked up. She is eight.
A black bearded trucker slows down
Claiming he'll call a trooper from ahead,
A second trucker stops,
Pulling us high up
Onto his driver's seat,
Taking us to the next concrete oasis.

Here the great beasts of burden stand,
Their drivers huddled for the night,
And in this caravansarai
My daughter and I wait for word
That our stranger's credit is good.

The world, for all our paths
And travels through it,
Still seems larger
Than we can make it tame,
Like the sky,
Where airplanes
Will never be
More than hopeful specks
Of campfire light,
In the heart-stopping dunes
Of some desert night.

Cradle Me In Colored Light

Black branched
Orange nebulae,
Blue autumn tree
Against noon sky,
Pinwheel of sun fire,
Blood orange, lemon yellow,
Soothe these tired eyes.
Peach parasol
Laced with dark wire,
Giant parachute,
Catch me once
Before I expire,
Hold me one day away
From winter.
Keep your bat-winged leaves,
Each sweet as children's paintings,
From falling on my throat,
Tributary to my eye,
Deep channeled river,
Cradle me in colored light.

PORTRAITS

Bindings
(for Edward Robbins)

My father,
Like so many other young Viennese Jews
Born into the 20th century,
Studied medicine instead of religion.
For him,
The rubber blood pressure tube
Around the arm,
Not the healing leather tongs
And Hebrew prayers of *Tefillin*.
And as I sat in his office,
A young Midwestern American boy
Lucky enough to have lived
To the middle of the century,
I felt him tie my arm,
Then wrap me,
Not in a silk prayer shawl,
But in the self-adhering
Arm band he inflated
To read my pressure on a gage,
Recording at what rate
My bursting blood escaped,
While I wondered what, about my heart,
This stern and conscientious man
Had come to know,
What he loved about his duty,
And what, about his duty,
Showed that he loved me.

Traveling Kit
(for my father)

An extra arch-support
For your right foot.
You had flat feet.
The curved black leather
Still shines like young skin.

An extra pair of glasses
With thick plastic frames,
You were nearly blind in one eye,
The left lens scratched.
Your dandruff still adheres
To the temples.
I try them on.
My head is now as large as yours,
Our eyes about the same,
Except by this time, you had bifocals.

The old-fashioned black hairnet
You brought from Vienna and used
Even after you lost most of your hair
Still smells strongly of Alberto VO5.
It made you look
Like a funny, slicked-down
Arabian sheik, after your shower.

The VO5 tube
Still has your imprint on it,
You squeezed from the top.
Your toothbrush in its cracked
Plastic case still smells of paste,
The bristles were wearing down,
And you were almost out
Of Ultra Brite.

Your Mennen's after-shave
Skin conditioner,
(You were always looking
For a better electric shaver),
Antiseptic ointment,
Dramamine for motion sickness,
Pills for colds and diarrhea,
Surgical lubricant, bandaids,
Noseguard against the sun, cologne,
Shirt-collar stay, penny,
Safety pin, broken rubber band.

In a separate compartment,
Your Ritalin: "In case of emergency,
I am receiving long-term anticoagulant
Therapy. If I am injured or threatened
With bleeding, take me to a hospital.
If I am able to swallow, give me two
Of the accompanying tablets
With some water."
The second shirt-collar stay,
Tie clips, cuff links, extra buttons,
Your calling card: Fritz Koenig, M.D.

Mother At The Museum

Mother,
You slept through the whole film,
A nodding, little old lady of whims.
I watched
Both the ghostly woman painter
And you,
My flickering, fading,
One-time creator.

She made,
Out of her body,
A bird from her eyebrows,
A broken, marble column from her spine,
Flowers from a breast,
A tree out of her heart,
Blood from a childless,
Arrow-pierced womb,
A world from her empty room.

Mother,
You slept through the whole film,
A nodding, little old lady of whims,
But to me
You are still the darkhaired beauty
Who created me
Out of your body.

Twin-Born
(for a brother)

Twin-born
Is still-born,
Bone-blood
Sacks of skin born,
Infants' first mourning cries,
Wind-born.

Brood-born
Is brother-torn,
Other-shorn,
Forlorn
Breast-wrested
Matadors.

Now,
Singe these mountain sparrows,
Heart-burst
Ghost-town geysers,
This blue morning,
Let them be quick-born.

Not Yet A Part
(for John Sanders)

When I was young,
I fell in love
With a blond farm girl.
I had just started grade school,
And she came in from the country
On a bus.

I lived in Catlin, Illinois,
With my parents
Just arrived from Vienna, Austria,
Driven out
For having dark hair and skin.
My twin brother,
For some reason, was fair,
And my father loved him
For his golden chance to fit in.

In this new land of yellow corn,
I worshipped Karen Cord.
She fit in everywhere, and every day,
Cloudy or clear,
Like the sun in the fields,
Like my brother in my father's fears,
Whereas I hovered in lunar shadow,
Waiting for someone
To reflect light on me.

And Karen of the fair skin
Did love me
For a while,
My black curls were a rarity
In her yellow world.
On the playground,
I would line up with her,
And shine when she laughed.

Until one day,
The yellow bus
Brought a new boy to our school.
He could do all the things I could do.
He could run fast.
And when he ran, his light brown hair
Flowed fine as corn silk.

Then Karen Cord sent a message:
She loved him more than me,
And suddenly
The merry-go-round stopped gliding
Like waves of corn in the wind.

It began to make me sea-sick,
Like an immigrant's freight boat,
Over-crowded with memories and dark,
Not a part of the world it came from
Or the world it came to,
Not yet a part.

The Present Life Presents

There she sits, my mother,
Posing in the ruins of Pompeii
In an old photograph,
In a 20's flapper dress,
Shop girl from Vienna, full of dreams,
Visiting her aunt in Rome,
Thinking, oh, those poor people,
Caught in the flow of the volcano
And turned to stone, caught in time,
Perpetually young or old, mimicking
Their own gestures of centuries ago!

Among those monkey-like,
Ash people, crouching
In low poses of life's everyday tableau,
Stale as yesterday's news
Two thousand years removed,
In this stone, wax-museum zoo,
Sits my mother, reclining in the ruin
Of my memory,
Her bobbed hair unmoved,
Reminding me, the past is what passes,
What does not pass is gall and stone,
Old photos, our own Pompeian ruins,
The present is the present life presents.

Lion Eyes

Green eyes,
You seem to rise
On slow sinew,
I see your
Taut cheek
Grown on proud bone,
Lion eyes,
Wherein
My brain
Takes mane.

Self Respect

Self respect,
Margaret calls it,
As she crawls back
Into her Southern shell
And fights the Civil War
All over again, every time
She drawls open her mouth,
And in her rebellious fight
The South always wins,
Or almost wins,
But comes out proud.

Cross between a Southern Belle
Come up North
And a bulging Buddha,
Margaret wears her womanhood heavily,
Like a mantle she did not seek,
Yet decorates her stocky body
With clothes too feminine,
Found by Margaret the scavenger,
In every second-hand store
From here to there.
Margaret's in my dreams again tonight,
And that's not rare.

Margaret, you carve yourself
By your own blunt hands
Out of your own shell,
Like the Chinese do
From Mother of Pearl.
I seem to see you sitting,
Part sage, part girl,
As though in stone,
Until, from the edges
Of your shell,
I notice you still are knitting
Your soft-hard world,
Your own wishing star,
Your earthly home.

Rose

Rose,
You who clean
My house on Thursdays,
Had your birthday party
In your Cicero storefront church.

Reverend Rose,
In your mother-white, ample dress
And triangle Sunday hat,
Rose of Africa,
Black and gallant,
Had our peoples met
On desert sands,
Mine from the Levant,
Tribesman and nomad,
Black and Jew,
You could have been my dark aunt.

Rose of Sharon and Sahara,
You who have held
More fire in your skin,
Mine burned from within,
Your poetry is old medicine.
Shake your spangled rattle,
Gap-toothed child of fifty-eight,
Woman of wise battle,
Laugh and play organ
While sisters writhe
On the healing floor,
Singing to be saved:
Give us roses, Lord, before the grave.

Twilight city,
Twilight land
And twilight world,
And me, Mother Rose,
Teach the kindness to be brave.

United Parcel
(for Joe)

You had it your way,
With shaggy old rabbi
(Scion of a dynasty)
And the handful of us stragglers
Weaving our cars behind your hearse
Through the weeds out back of O'Hare,
Past the Air Freight
And Air Cargo signs,
Your last wish, to be buried in Israel.

At American Airlines'
Deserted loading dock
We struggled with you,
In your crate marked "Human Remains,"
"Handle with Care,"
The one end stamped "Head,"
Staggered under your weight
As the wind whipped us
Against your coffin,

Which rises on a lift truck,
That pivots like a bored athlete
And drives mechanically toward the goal.
But the man who survived
German death march
Does not fear a solitary ride
From Chicago to Jerusalem
In the hold of a plane,
His way,
As a United Parcel.

Wheelchair
(for Jason)

To live on a wheel
Seems Medieval,
A torture
Of misshapenness,
The racking of a body
Less God's grace.

Yet to live on a wheeled chair
Means always to rest
On the shape of a seal,
God's agreement sealed,
A round stamp
Of final importance
On a document of testimony,
That all life moves by turning,
Like the earth.

All that moves one way
Will soon move the other,
The bent in shape
Will soon seem straight,
As lost connections
Encircle perfection,
The simple of mind
May be most wise,
And the longest seated
May be first to rise.

The Baccarat Caller

Place your bets . . . .
Are there any more bets . . . ?
. . . Cards, please.

Players show natural nine.
There will be no draws . . . .
. . . Players win, nine over two.

Pay the players!
Shoe moves, chair two.
We have a new bank.

Place your bets . . . .
Are there any more bets . . . ?
. . . Cards, please.

Players show three.
Bank shows two.
Card for the players.
Card for the bank, seven to beat.

Players win, seven over two.
Pay the players!
Shoe moves, chair three.
We have a new bank.

Place your bets . . . .
Are there any more bets . . . ?
. . . Cards, please.

Players show four,
Bank wins with a natural nine.
Place your bets . . . .
Are there any more bets . . . ?
. . . Cards, please.

IMMORTALITIES

Inside His Own Black Eyes

A window-box of mottled shadow-flowers
Warm and white,
On the bare wall near my bed,
First strong Spring light,

As I,
A sad boy,
Would sometimes stop and look
At nothing but the bright.

As first eyeball
Of first fish
Saw through cold water-wall
Of night.

As, after a massacre,
Survivors have grown hopeful
Over coals
Of fire.

As Buddha,
Awakening,
Must have found paradise
Inside his own black eyes.

Every Deep Pool Our Farthest Wish

Any mother of mine,
Humming any lovely tune,
You hold me in the swimming pool,
Cradling your friend,
Your anxious fool,
Seeming to speak:

Be what you always wanted to be,
A poet, a painter,
It's all the same with me,
For every earthworm
May become a starfish,
And every deep pool
Our farthest wish.

Dad, You Died Abourning

With no warning,
Dad, you died abourning,
Giving birth, I see,
To you and me.

Dad, I want to cradle you
As mothers with their children do,
Fathers need a cradling,
And sons can when they learn to sing.

Flower House

We are not ready
For the giant conservatory,
Magnificent glass growth
In a decaying neighborhood,

Monument to some forgotten belief
In the dignity of plant
And animal meetings,
Streamlined,
As the style was then,
A vast airplane hanger
For housing light.

Inside we find
The Mediterranean in May,
A tracery wilderness of greens,
Air sweet and moist as first love,
Fountains bathing statues
Through girdered arches.

And everywhere plants,
So many one could believe
There was a god
Partial to green.

We walk through rooms
From tropic to desert,
Orchids purple with love
To crop trees of coffee and coconut,

Until finally the plant world ends,
And we are back,
Like Adam and Eve,
The first pair
Again in the first room,

Walking by the white statue
Of lovers called Idyll.
This has been a dreaming time
In a deserted mausoleum,
Where vegetation thrives
Though culture has fled,

Shared with only a vagrant
Feeding bread to resident squirrels,
A white couple chic and in love,
A black guard reading the paper
In the greenhouse wheelchair,

A conservatory for dreams,
Of a time before Cain and Able fought
And Job was empoverished,
The warm, green world
Where all come back to this,
When houses were made of flowers.

The Poet, Wildest Of Animals

Untameable,
The poet, wildest of animals,
Incapable of being truly domesticated,
Dies quickly in captivity
Like an African or Australian bushman,
Roams free
From the time it leaves its mother,
Does not seem subject
To the rules of most animals
But lives by a rule of its own.
Hunts primarily alone,
But returns stealthily to its lair
For food and rest and comfort
From its kind.
Defends itself by its ability
To make leaps
From one narrow
And apparently inescapable place
To another,
And by its blinding speed
When faced with danger.

Beautiful to watch from a distance
Though rarely sighted today,
Being killed off in ever greater numbers
By the over-crowded city
That is the world,
Sometimes seen lying
Crushed on the pavement,
Still occasionally found
Living in the mountains
Or, rarely,
Trapped in hiding between high buildings.

Once roamed free
In jungles of Africa and South America,
Plains of Asia, valleys of Europe,
Deserts of the Middle East,
Forests of North America, Arctic fields.
In primitive legend,
Said to be returning one day
To lead the peoples,
Through glimpses of its defiant wildness,
To freedom.

Spirit Sailing

He hoists the prayer sail
Over his head,
Settles its fringed rigging
Around his shoulders,
Hears the gentle flap
Of wool canvas about his ankles,
A thousand year old commandment
To wrap himself in this shawl.
Each morning he sets sail,
Or sometimes rows
When he finds no hope of wind,
Taking commands in ancient Hebrew,
A vessel steering and being steered,
He draws the sail sheet over his eyes,
Out at dawn into a world of white,
Sailing within, and toward the light.

Spider Line

Spider line,
Sighted along the eye
At sunrise,
Tree web
In early morning tide,
Catch me before I grow blind,

Each day losing sight,
I tightrope on your fine sun filament,
A daylight firefly,
For a few seconds
I shine.

Silent, solar telephone wire,
Call and tell me
Before I grow deaf
How to be harmoniously singed,

From whom to get,
Like these light-streamed leaves,
The sunny, humming,
Silhouette of wings.

Rocking Horses Into Jerusalem

When the temple in Jerusalem
Is finally rebuilt,
I will have my red,
Wooden hobbyhorse back,
My brother will have his,
And we will rock
Until the robins fly in
Through the leaded glass windows again
On mysterious red-breasted light,
Spinning faster and faster
Over our heads
Until amidst our father's laughter
The doorframes fly up
And reassemble
Around the holy of holies,
The secret place
Where Abraham almost sacrificed Isaac,
A punishment
We will be sure no one deserves,
And Mother will come from the kitchen
With something to keep us til dinner,
And after we eat we will fall asleep,
Dreaming the new day to come,
As we ride our rocking horses
Into Jerusalem.

INDEX OF FIRST LINES

Index of First Lines

Green Whistle is set in a version of Times Roman.
It is sewn in signatures and printed on
acid-free paper in accord with the desire of
Wm Caxton Ltd to produce books of lasting
quality and attractiveness.